Piano Major Blues

**Playing Major Blues Scales & Songs on the Piano
for Moderate Level Pianists**

Copyright 2015
by
Kevin G. Pace

PaceMusicServices.com

Piano Major Blues

Playing Major Blues Scales & Songs on the Piano
for Moderate Level Pianists

Copyright 2015 by Kevin G. Pace

PaceMusicServices.com

Major Blues Scales

The Major Blues Scale is a six-note scale. It is the 1st Inversion of the Minor Blues scale. For example:

A Minor Blues:	A	C	D	Eb	E	G	A
C Major Blues:		C	D	Eb	E	G	A	C

It is also like the Major Pentatonic Mode with an added #2 or b3.

Half steps between scale degrees are as follows: 2-1-1-3-2-3.

Some chords that may be used with this scale are as follows: (examples in C Blues Major)

Dominant 7 chord (C-E-G-Bb)

Dominant 9 chord (C-E-G-Bb-D)

Minor 6 chord (C-Eb-G-A)

Dominant 13(no 11) chord (C-E-G-Bb-D-A)

Major 7 built chord (C-E-G-B)

Major 9 built chord (C-E-G-B-D)

Major 6 chord (C-E-G-A)

Here are some ways to think about the Blues Major scale:

1-Think of the half steps between scale degrees: 2   1   1   3   2   3

2-Play a Major Pentatonic scale with an added #2 or b3. For example:

C Major Pentatonic Scale:	C	D		E	G	A	C
C Major Blues scale:	C	D	Eb	E	G	A	C

3-Play a Major Scale, but use only scale degrees 1-2-3-5-6. Then add a #2 or b3. For example:

C Major Scale:	C	D	E	~~F~~	G	A	~~B~~	C
Scale degree:	1	2	b3	3		5	6		1
C Major Blues scale:	C	D	Eb	E		G	A		C

Here are the 12 Major Blues scales
with possible fingerings:

Alternate fingerings

Hand								Alternate fingerings
RH	1	2	3	1	2	3	1/5	
	C	D	Eb	E	G	A	C	
LH	5/1	4	3	2	1	2	1	
RH	2	3	1	2	3	1	2	
	Db	Eb	E	F	Ab	Bb	Db	
LH	4/1	3	2	1	3	2	1	
RH	2	3	1	2	3	1	2	1-2-3-4-1-2-1
	D	E	F	Gb	A	B	D	
LH	5/1	4	3	2	1	2	1	
RH	2	3	4	1	2	1	2	3-1-3-1-3-1-3
	Eb	F	Gb	G	Bb	C	Eb	
LH	2	1	4	3	2	1	2	
RH	1	2	3	4	1	2	1/3	3-4-1-2-1-2-3
	E	F#	G	G#	B	C#	E	
LH	5/1	4	3	2	1	2	1	
RH	1	2	3	1	2	3	1/5	
	F	G	Ab	A	C	D	F	
LH	5/1	4	3	2	1	2	1	
RH	2	3	1	2	3	1	2	
	Gb	Ab	A	Bb	Db	Eb	Gb	
LH	3/1	2	1	4	3	2	1	
RH	2	3	4	1	2	1	2	1-2-3-1-2-3-1
	G	A	Bb	B	D	E	G	
LH	5/1	4	3	2	1	2	1	
RH	2	3	1	2	3	1	2	
	Ab	Bb	B	C	Eb	F	Ab	
LH	3	2	1	3	2	1	3	
RH	1	2	3	4	1	2	1/3	
	A	B	C	C#	E	F#	A	
LH	5/1	4	3	2	1	2	1	2-1-3-2-1-3-2
RH	4/2	1	2	1	2	3	4	4-1-2-3-1-2-4
	Bb	C	Db	D	F	G	Bb	
LH	2	1	4	3	2	1	2	
RH	1	3	1	2	3	4	1/5	1-2-1-2-3-4-1
	B	C#	D	D#	F#	G#	B	
LH	3/1	2	1	4	3	2	1	

This book is organized in the following manner in all 12 keys: RH scale, LH scale, both hands scale, a review of three RH scales together, and a song using the scale. All music is intended to give examples of how to incorporate these scales into musical compositions or improvisations.

Explanation of Chords

The Major Blues scale is generally used along with the following chords:
-Dominant 7 chords
-Major 7 chords
-Major 6 chords
-Minor 6 chords

Here are some samples of chords that could be used with the Major Blues Scale (examples are in C):

Dominant 7:	C	E	G	Bb
Major 7:	C	E	G	B
Major 6:	C	E	G	A
Minor 6:	C	Eb	G	A

The root of the chord generally matches the 1st scale degree. For example, if a C Major Blues scale is being played, then generally one of the above mentioned chords in C would be used. If an F Major Blues scale is being played, then an F chord would generally be used.

Here's an example. Let's say we're playing a blues song using a I-IV-V chord progression in the key of C. When a C chord is played, a C Major Blues scale would generally be played. When an F chord is played, an F Major Blues scale would be played. When a G chord is played, a G Major Blues scale is used.

The 12 songs included in this book attempt to show this concept. Blues songs often use a I-IV-V chord pattern, although other chords can be used. The songs in this book are based on Major Blues scales, although notes outside the scale are sometimes used for artistic purposes.

C Major Blues RH Scale

Kevin G. Pace

C Major Blues LH Scale

Kevin G. Pace

PaceMusicServices.com

C Major Blues Both Hands Scale

Kevin G. Pace

G Major Blues RH Scale

Kevin G. Pace

G Major Blues LH Scale

Kevin G. Pace

G Major Blues Both Hands Scale

Kevin G. Pace

F Major Blues RH Scale

Kevin G. Pace

F Major Blues LH Scale

Kevin G. Pace

F Major Blues Both Hands Scale

Kevin G. Pace

C, F, G Major Blues RH Scale

Kevin G. Pace

Major Omar

(C Major Blues)

Kevin G. Pace

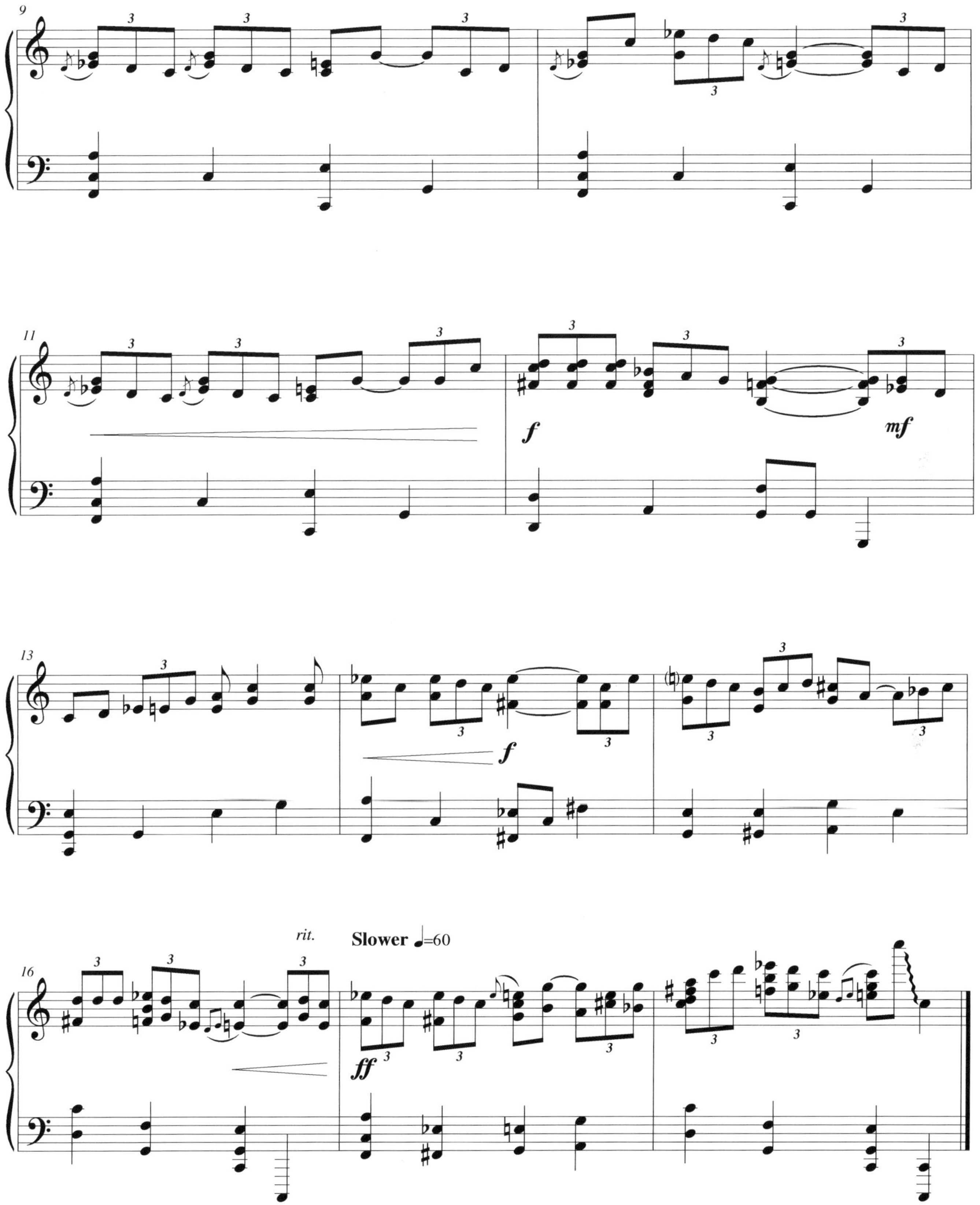
rit.
Slower ♩=60

D Major Blues RH Scale

Kevin G. Pace

D Major Blues LH Scale

Kevin G. Pace

D Major Blues Both Hands Scale

Kevin G. Pace

G, D, C Major Blues RH Scale

A Grand
(G Major Blues)

Kevin G. Pace

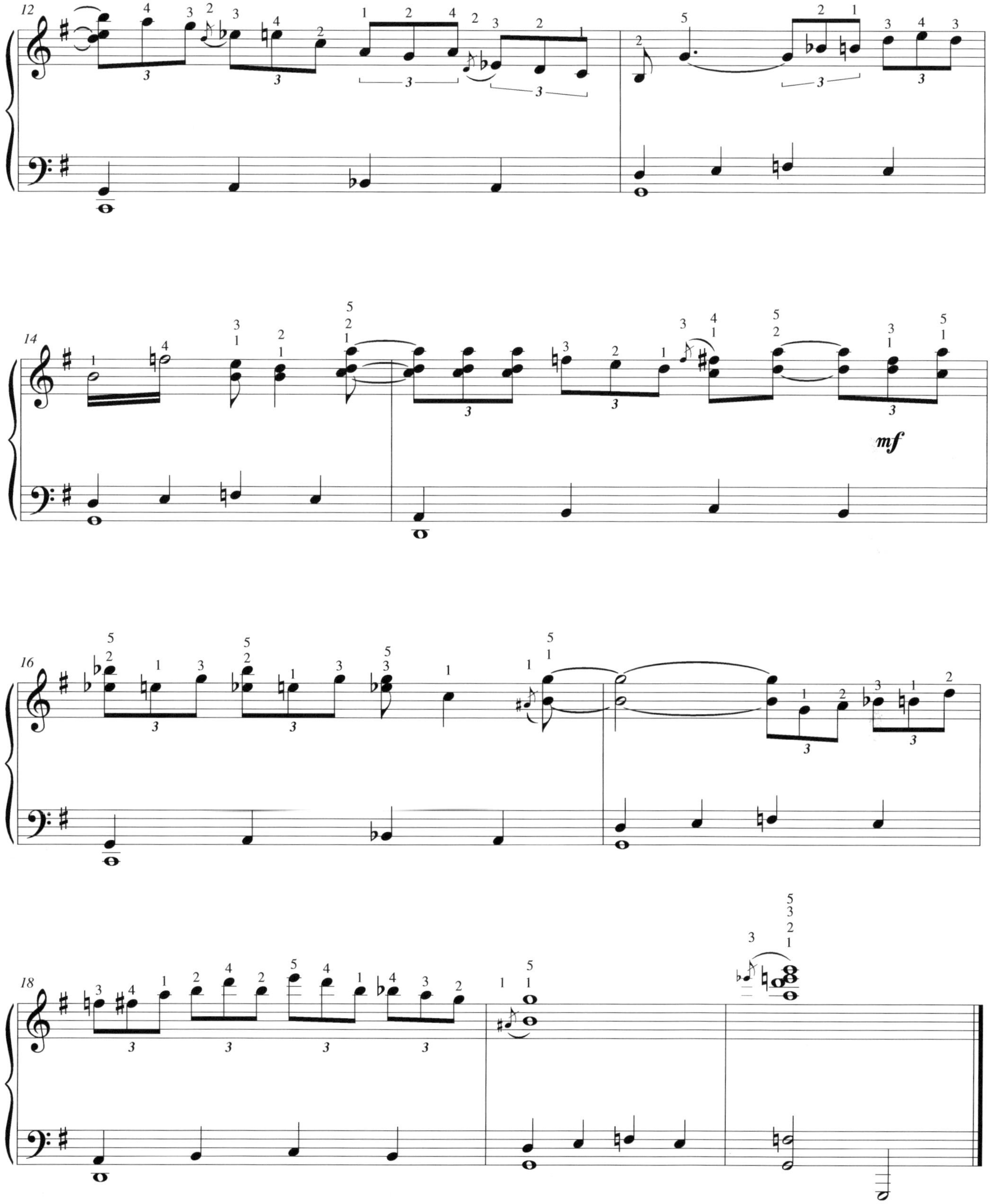
12
14
mf
16
18

A Major Blues RH Scale

Kevin G. Pace

A Major Blues LH Scale

Kevin G. Pace

A Major Blues Both Hands Scale

Kevin G. Pace

D, G, A Major Blues RH Scale

Kevin G. Pace

Cairn Gorm

(D Major Blues)

Kevin G. Pace

Straight Eighths ♩=132

LH plays the Major Blues scale
without the 2nd scale degree.

RH plays mainly the notes
of the Major Blues scale.

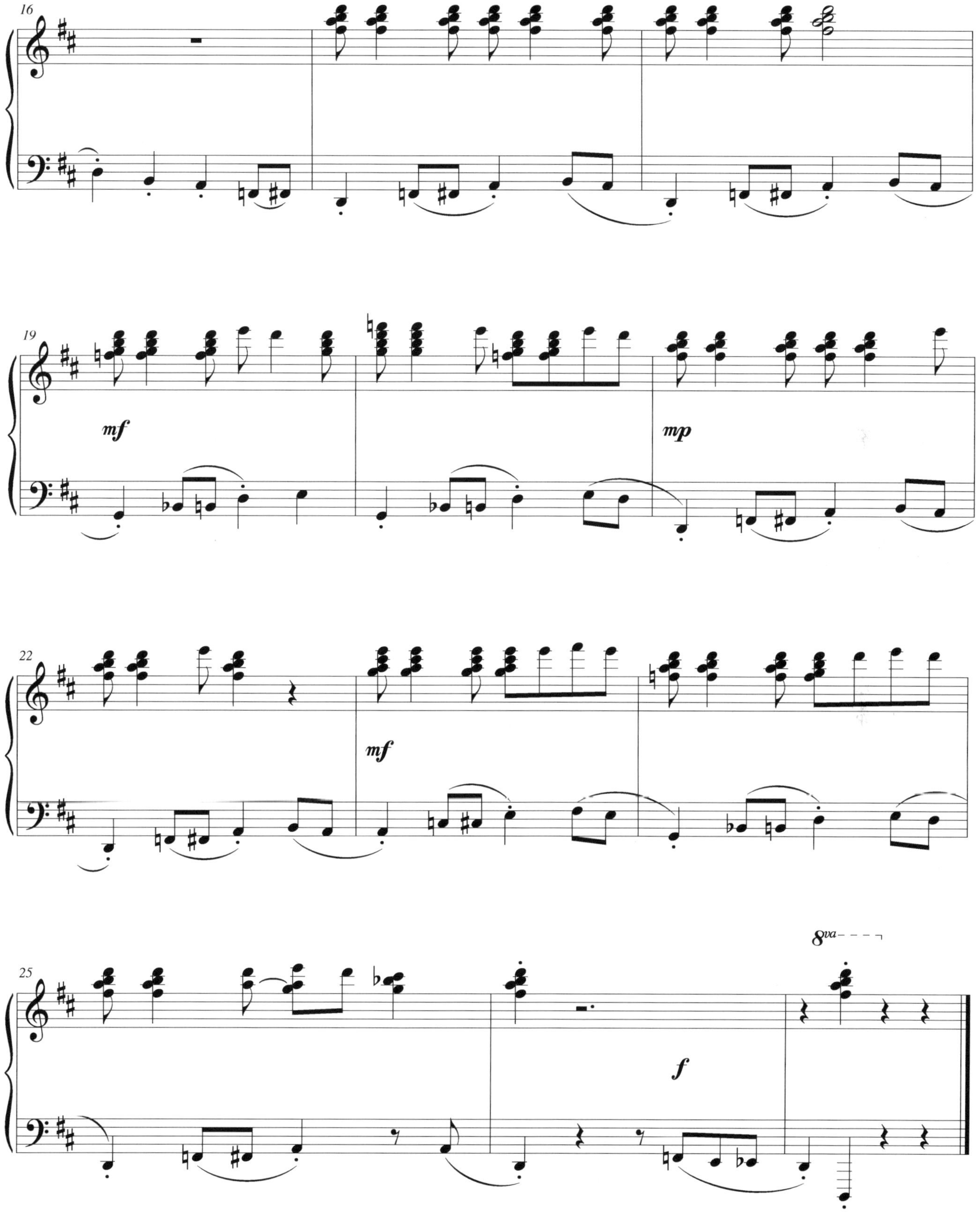
16
19
mf
mp
22
mf
8va
25
f

E Major Blues RH Scale

Kevin G. Pace

E Major Blues LH Scale

Kevin G. Pace

E Major Blues Both Hands Scale

Kevin G. Pace

A, D, E Major Blues RH Scale

Kevin G. Pace

Arkansas

(A Major Blues)

Kevin G. Pace

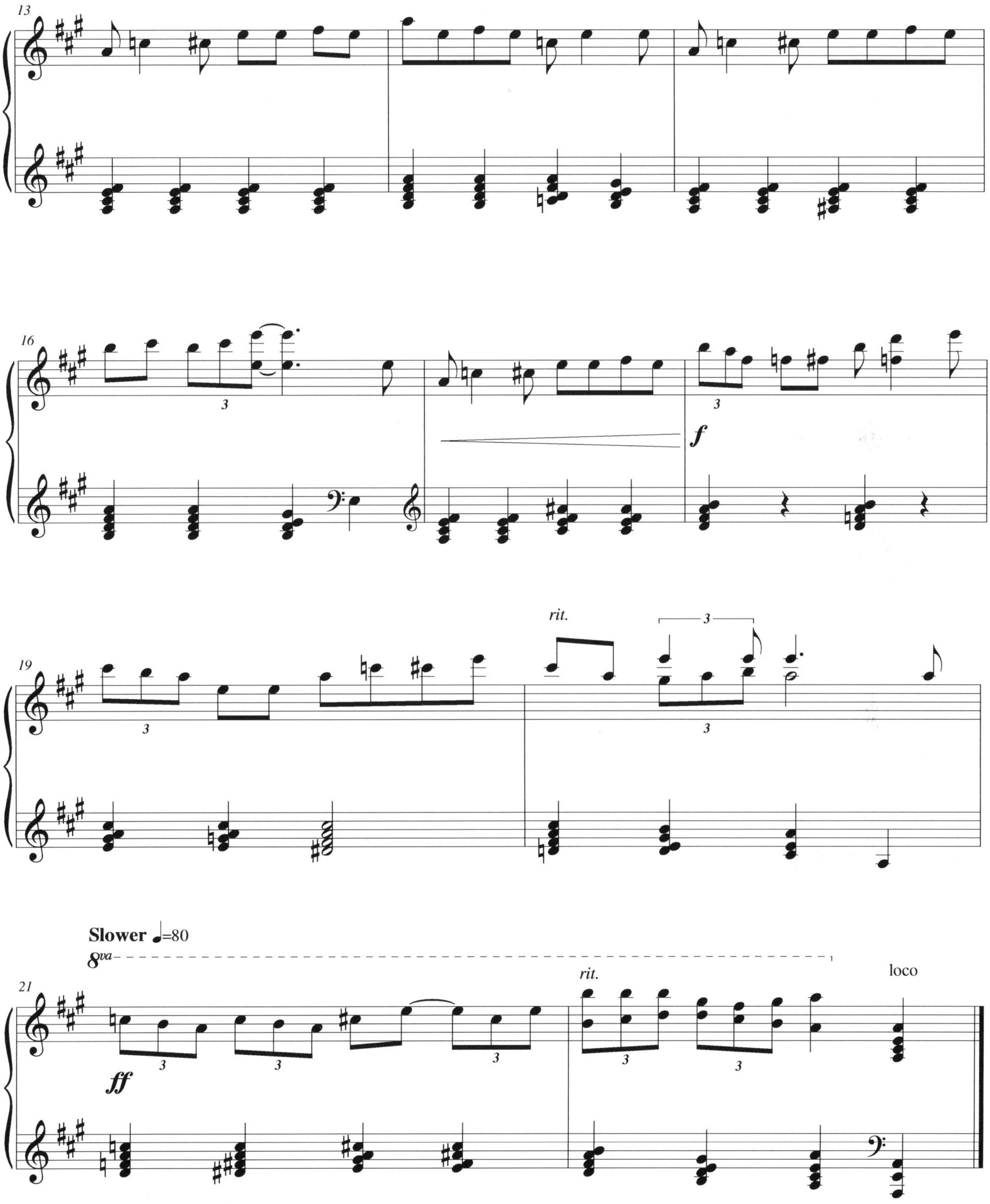
13
16
f
19
rit.
Slower ♩=80
8va
21
ff
rit.
loco

B Major Blues RH Scale

Kevin G. Pace

B Major Blues LH Scale

Kevin G. Pace

B Major Blues Both Hands Scale

Kevin G. Pace

E, A, B Major Blues RH Scale

Kevin G. Pace

Euler's Number
(E Major Blues)

This piece has been analyzed
for your edification.

Kevin G. Pace

The Roman numerals refer to the scale degree on which
the chords are built (these are in reference to the E Major scale).

This is called a tonicization. It is
read 5-7 of 4. This is the V7 chord
in A (the chord that comes next).

IV   **iv**   **Cad6/4**   **V7**   **I**   **VII7/IV**

This is called a tonicization. It is read 7-7 of 4. This is the VII7 chord in A (the chord that comes next).

IV   **iv**   **I**   **iv**   **V7**   **I**   **V7/IV**

IV   **iv**   **V7/vi**   **vi**

molto rit.

E Major Blues scale

V7/V   **V7**   **I**

F# Major Blues RH Scale

Kevin G. Pace

F# Major Blues LH Scale

Kevin G. Pace

F# Major Blues Both Hands Scale

Kevin G. Pace

B-E-F# Major Blues RH Scale

Kevin G. Pace

Free Flight
(B Major Blues)

Kevin G. Pace

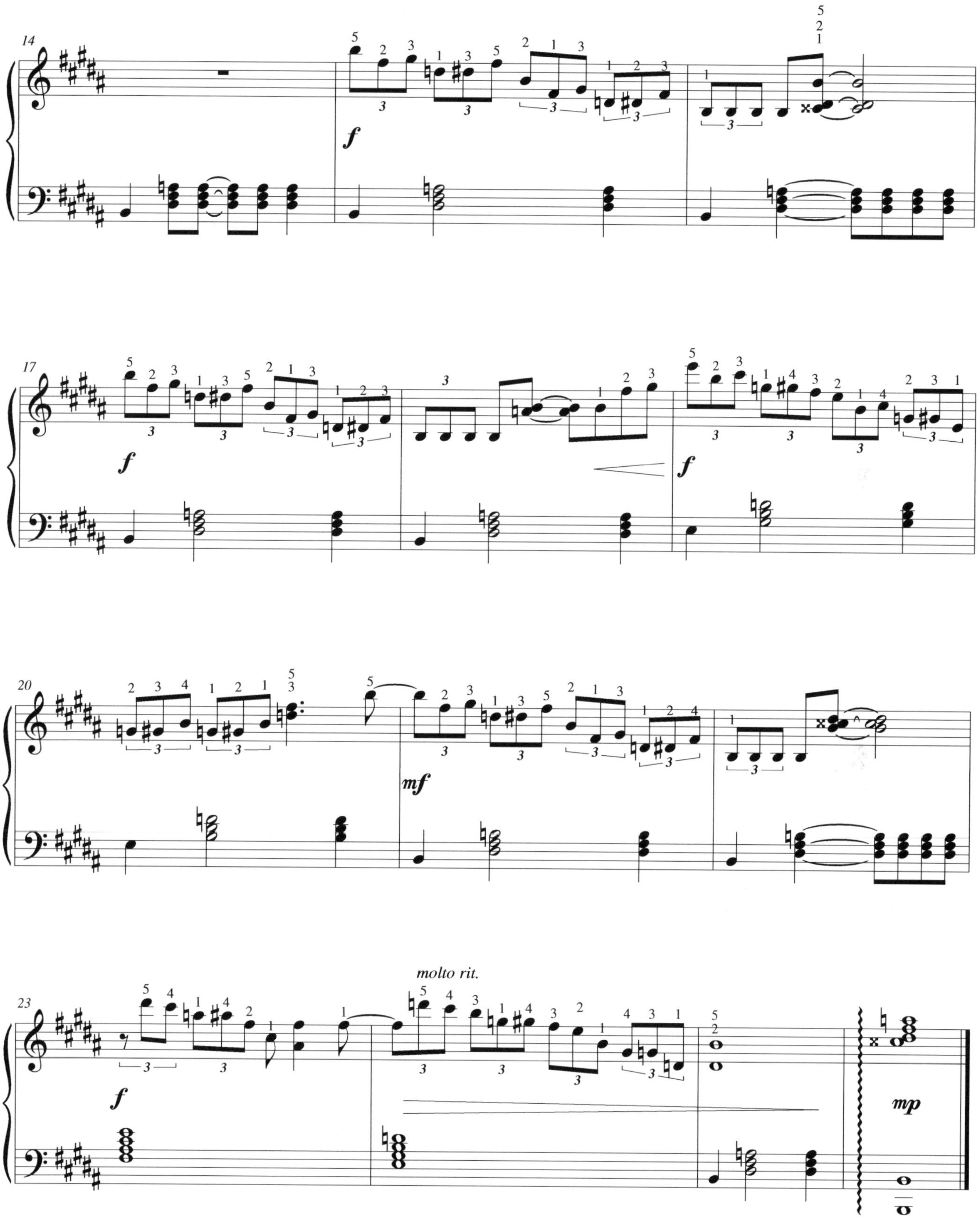
molto rit.

C# Major Blues RH Scale

Kevin G. Pace

C# Major Blues LH Scale

Kevin G. Pace

C# Major Blues Both Hands Scale

Kevin G. Pace

F#-B-C# Major Blues RH Scale

Kevin G. Pace

Python

(F# Major Blues)

Kevin G. Pace

Swing ♩=80

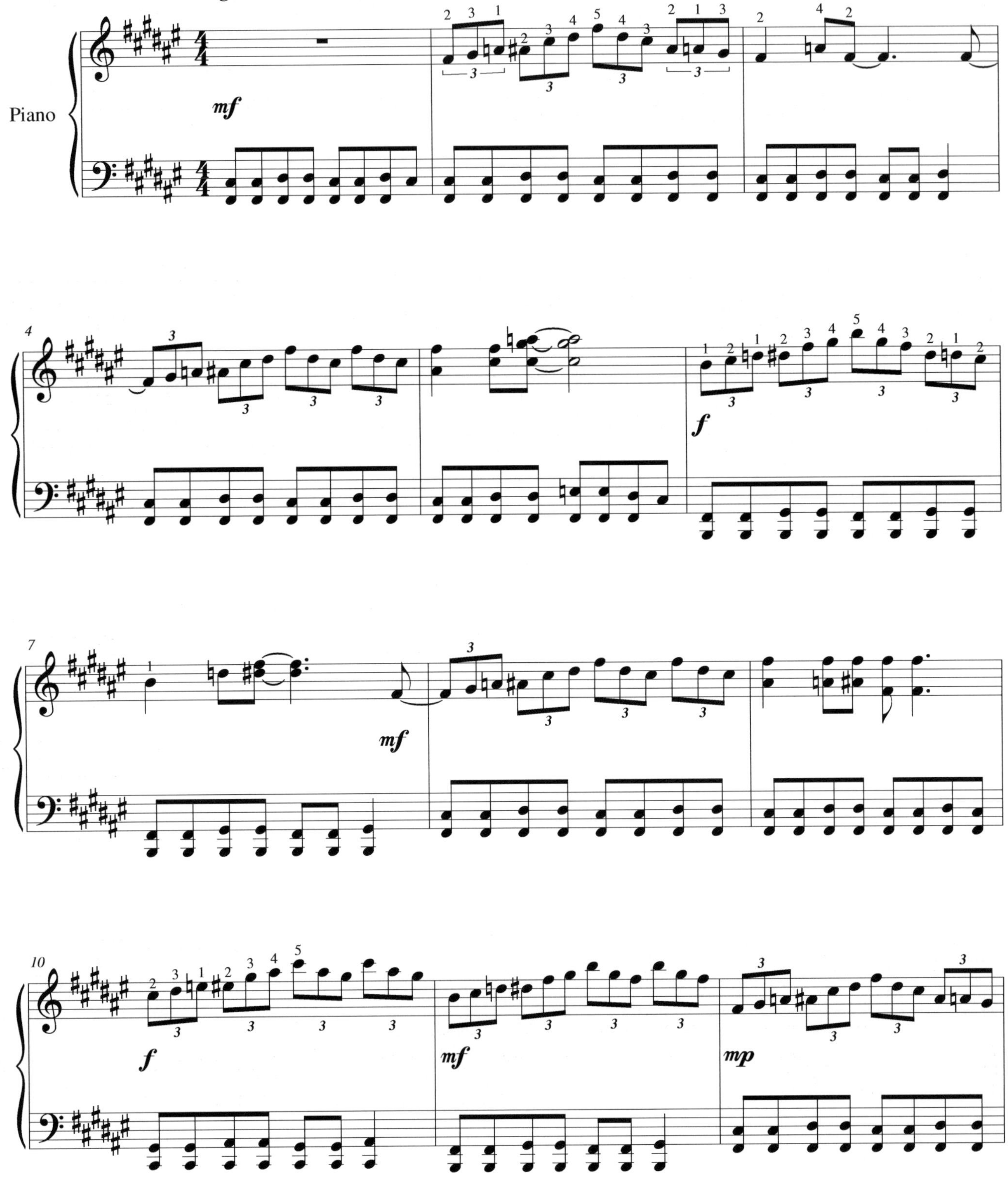

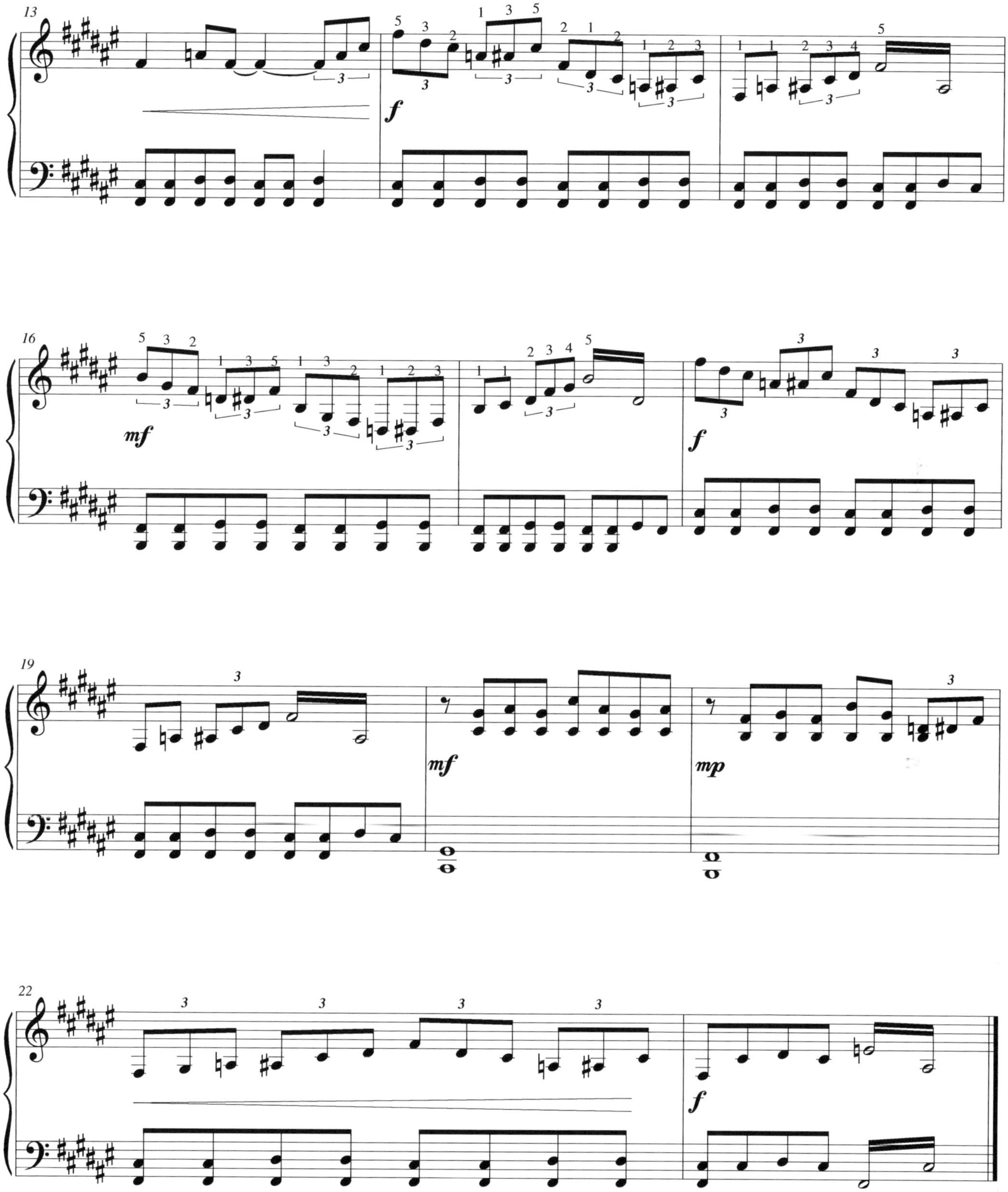
13
f
16
mf
f
19
mf
mp
22
f

Ab Major Blues RH Scale

Kevin G. Pace

Ab Major Blues LH Scale

Kevin G. Pace

Ab Major Blues Both Hands Scale

Kevin G. Pace

Db-Gb-Ab Major Blues RH Scale

Kevin G. Pace

Dubnium

(Db Major Blues)

Kevin G. Pace

PaceMusicServices.com

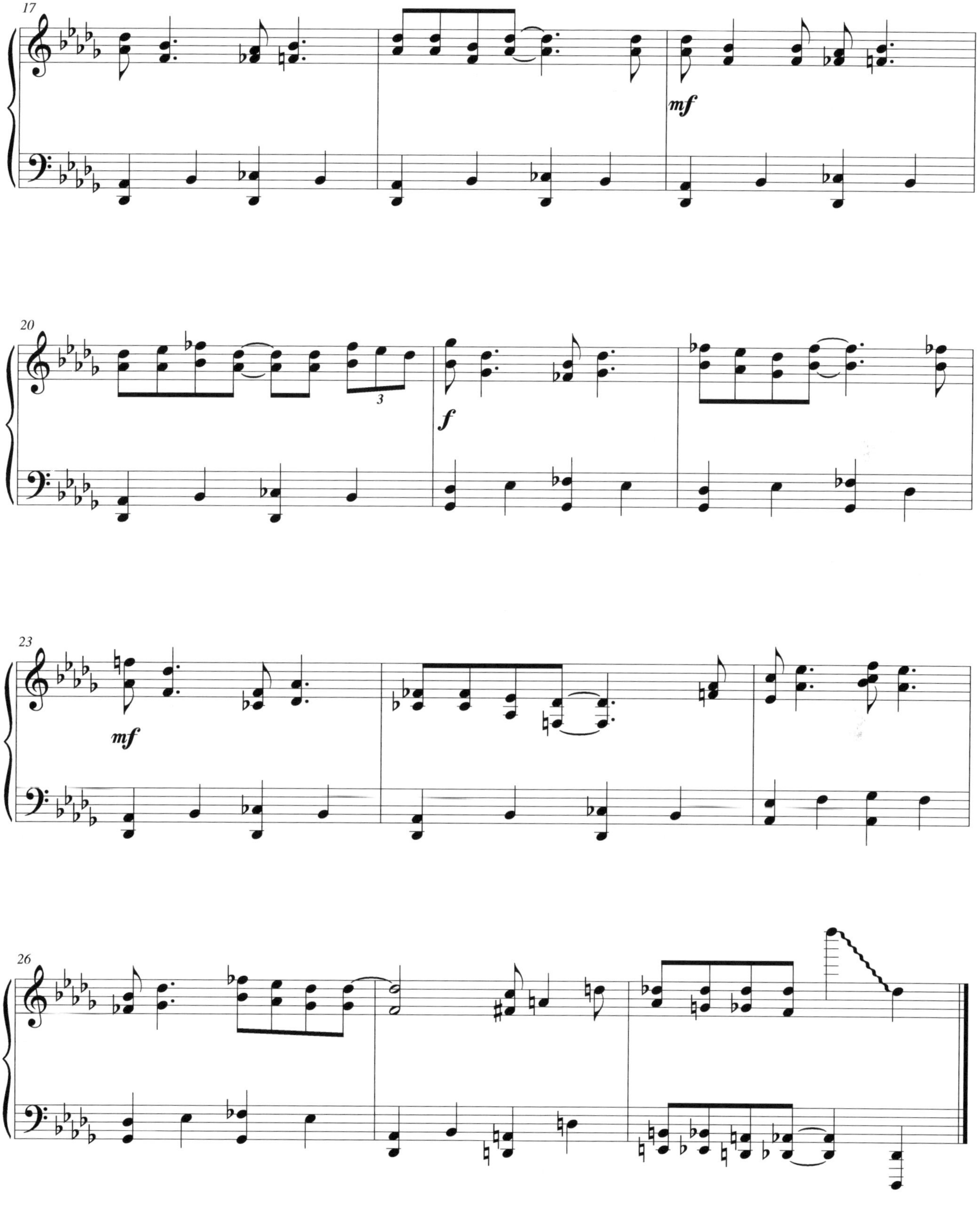
17
mf
20
3
f
23
mf
26

Eb Major Blues RH Scale

Kevin G. Pace

Eb Major Blues LH Scale

Kevin G. Pace

Eb Major Blues Both Hands Scale

Kevin G. Pace

Piano

One octave

Two octaves

Ab-Db-Eb Major Blues RH Scale

Kevin G. Pace

Dog Bones

(Ab Major Blues)

Kevin G. Pace

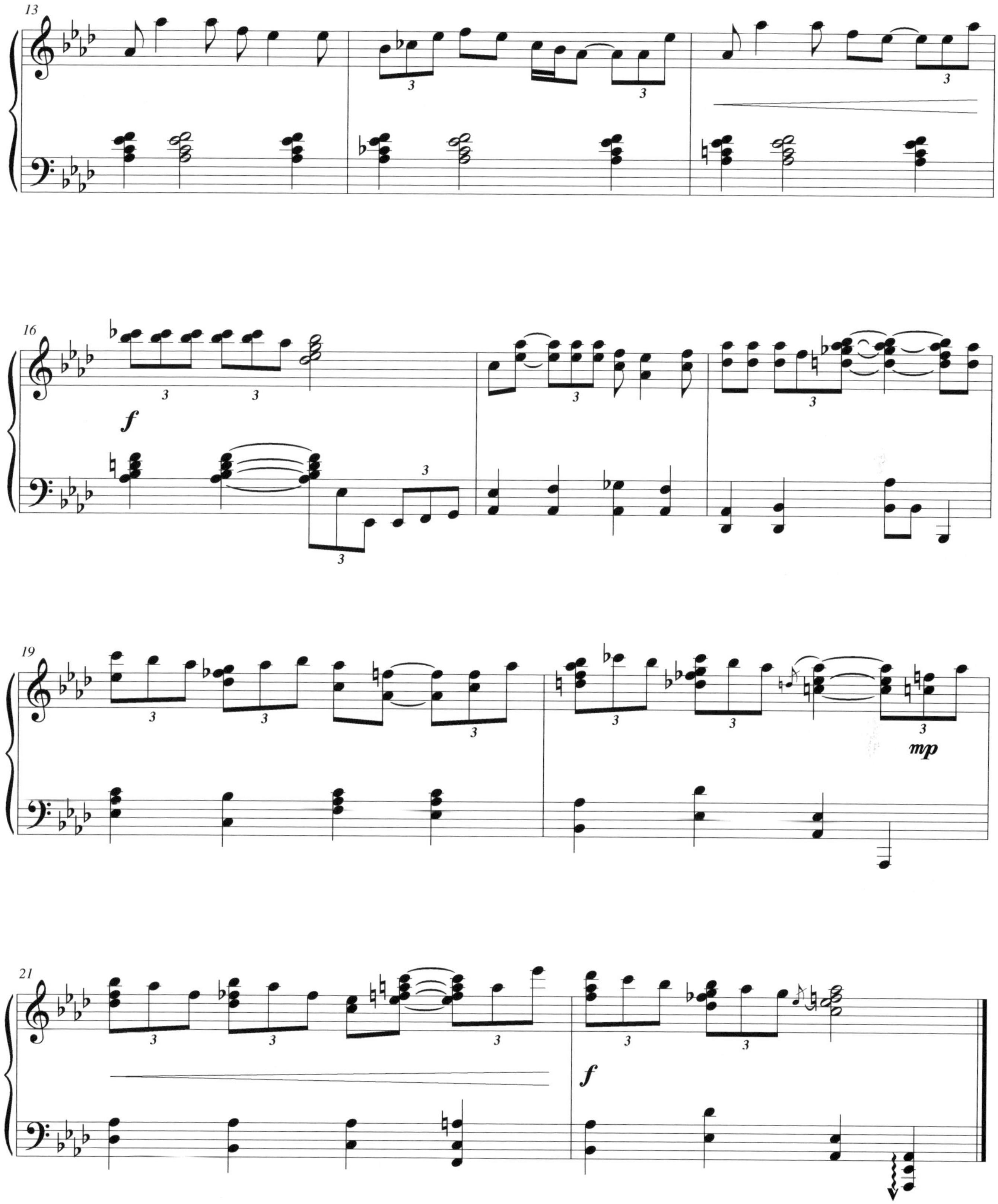
13
3
3
3
16
3
3
f
3
3
3
3
19
3
3
3
3
3
3
3
mp
21
3
3
3
3
3
f

Bb Major Blues RH Scale

Kevin G. Pace

Bb Major Blues LH Scale

Kevin G. Pace

Bb Major Blues Both Hands Scale

Kevin G. Pace

Eb-Ab-Bb Major Blues RH Scale

Kevin G. Pace

The Early Bird

(Eb Major Blues)

Kevin G. Pace

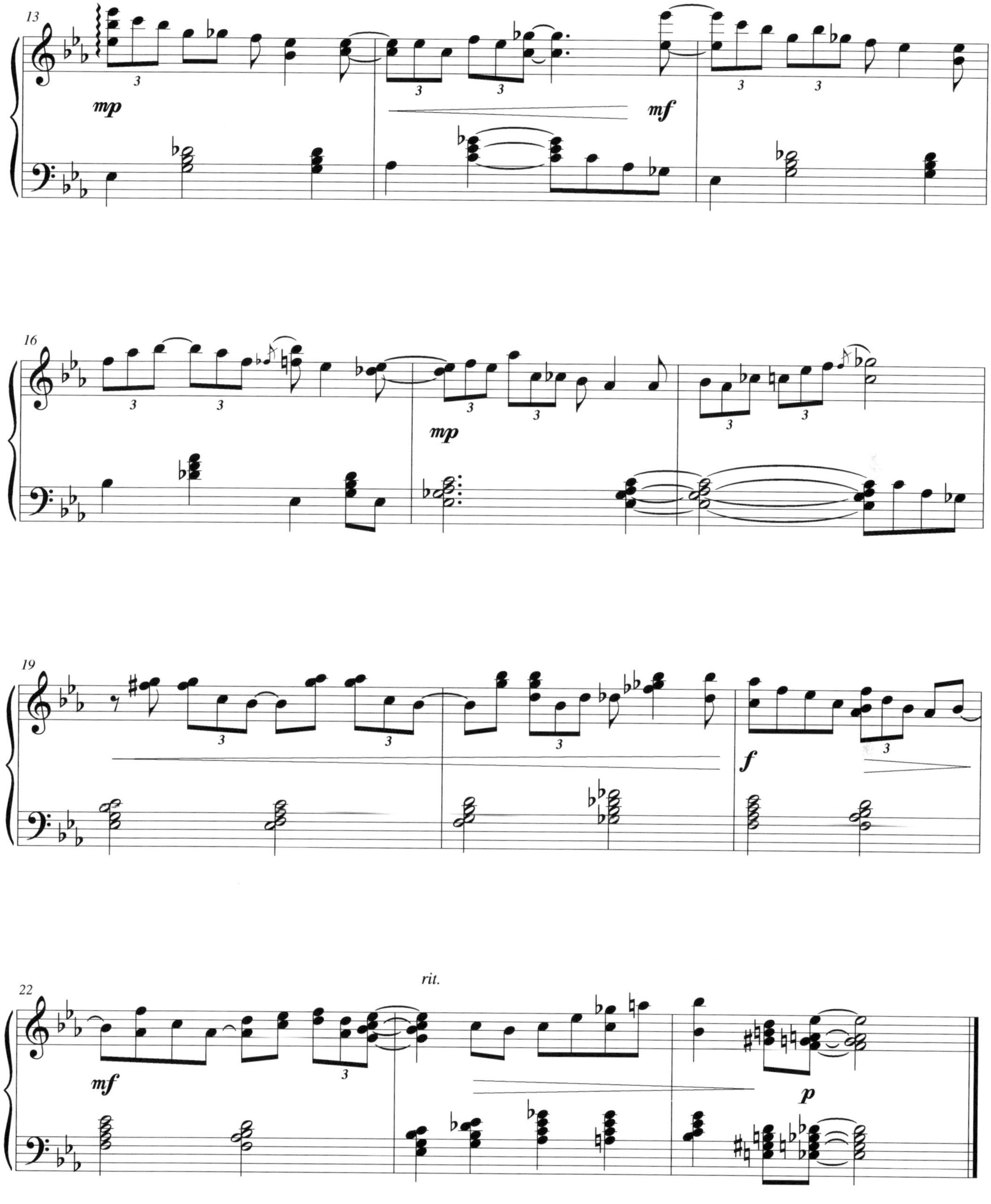
13
mp
mf
16
mp
19
f
22
rit.
mf
p

Bb-Eb-F Major Blues RH Scale

Kevin G. Pace

Pancakes

(Bb Major Blues)

Kevin G. Pace

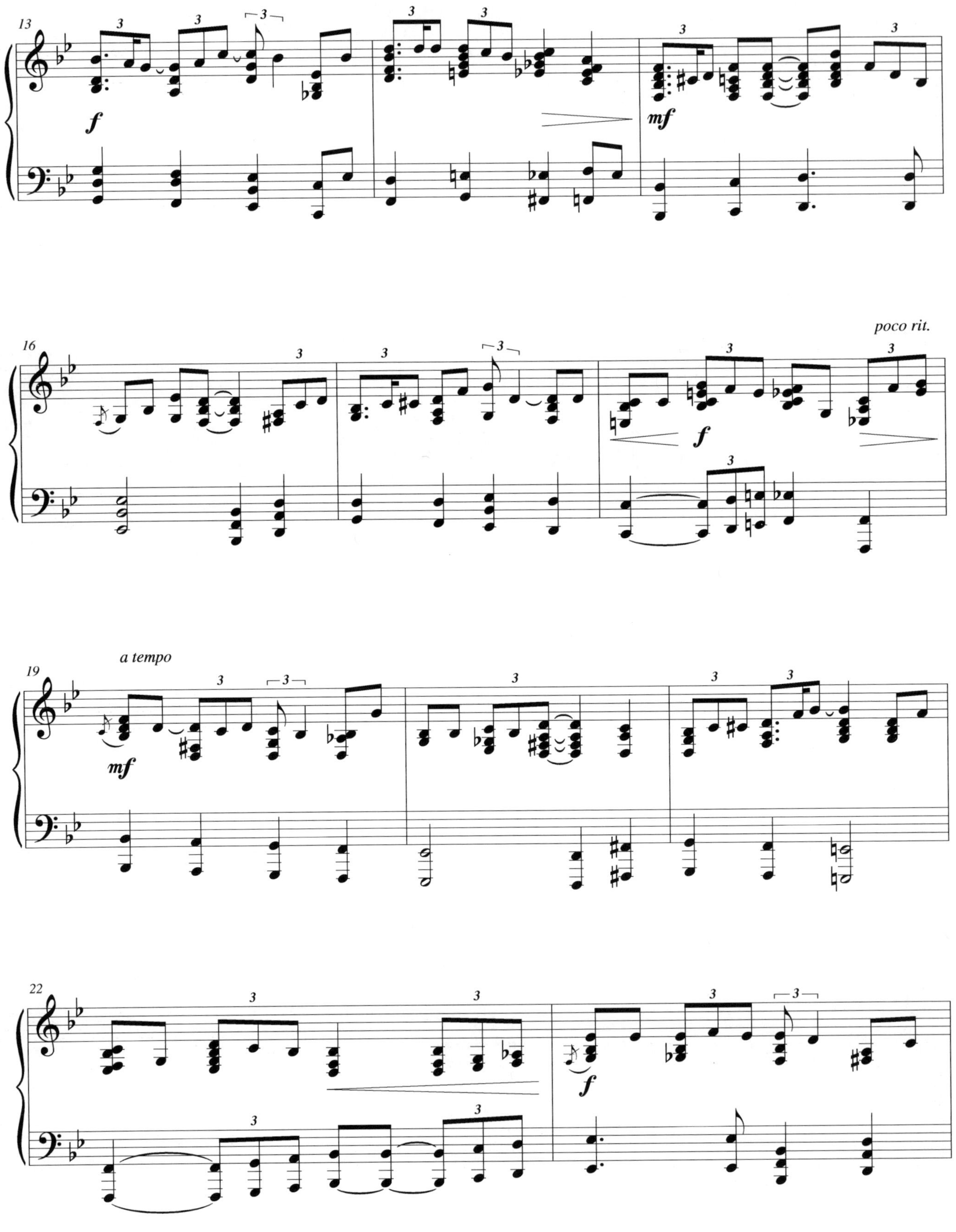
poco rit.
a tempo

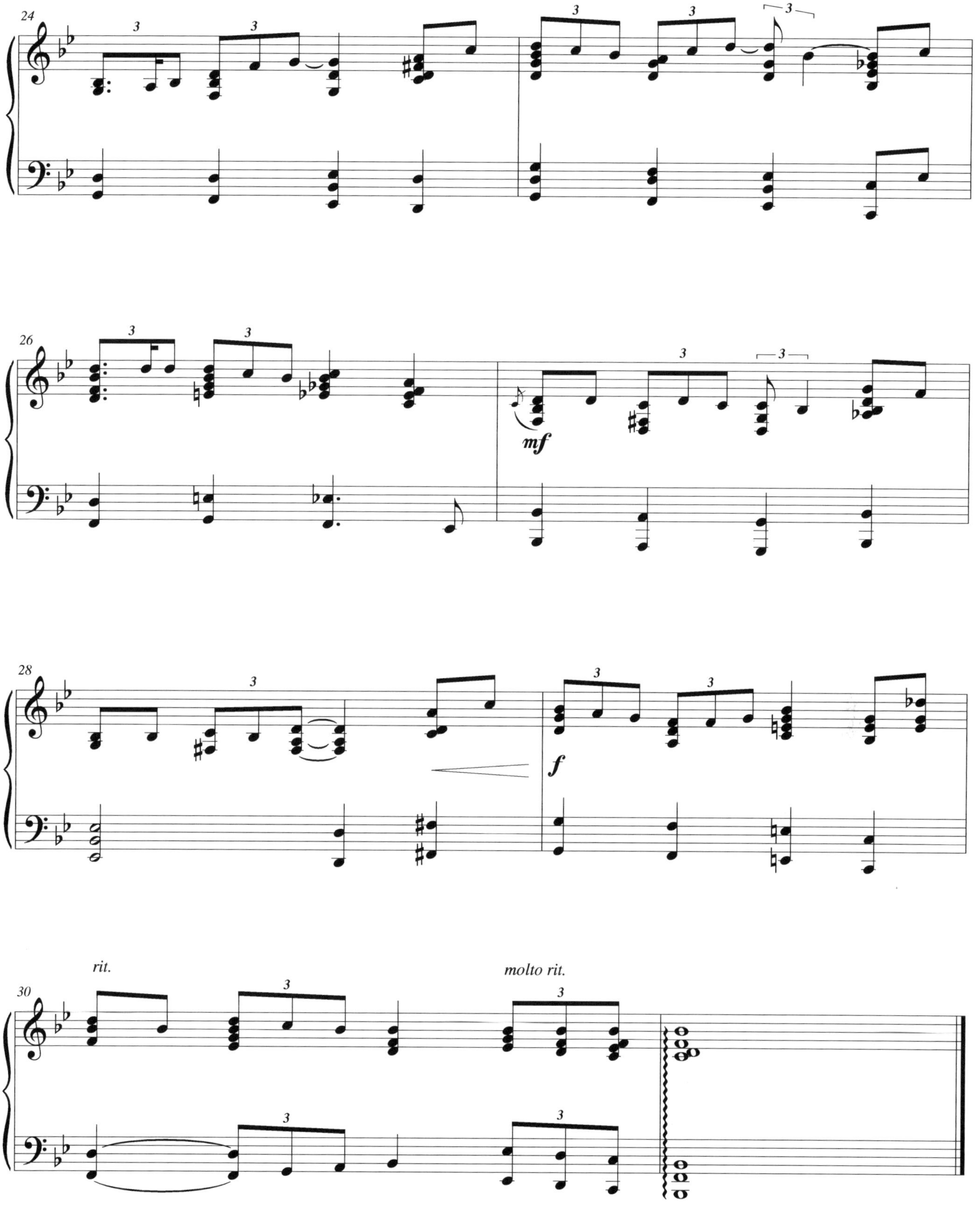
24
26
mf
28
f
30
rit.
molto rit.

F-Bb-C Major Blues RH Scale

Kevin G. Pace

In Effigy

(F Major Blues)

Kevin G. Pace

Straight eighths ♩=66

Piano

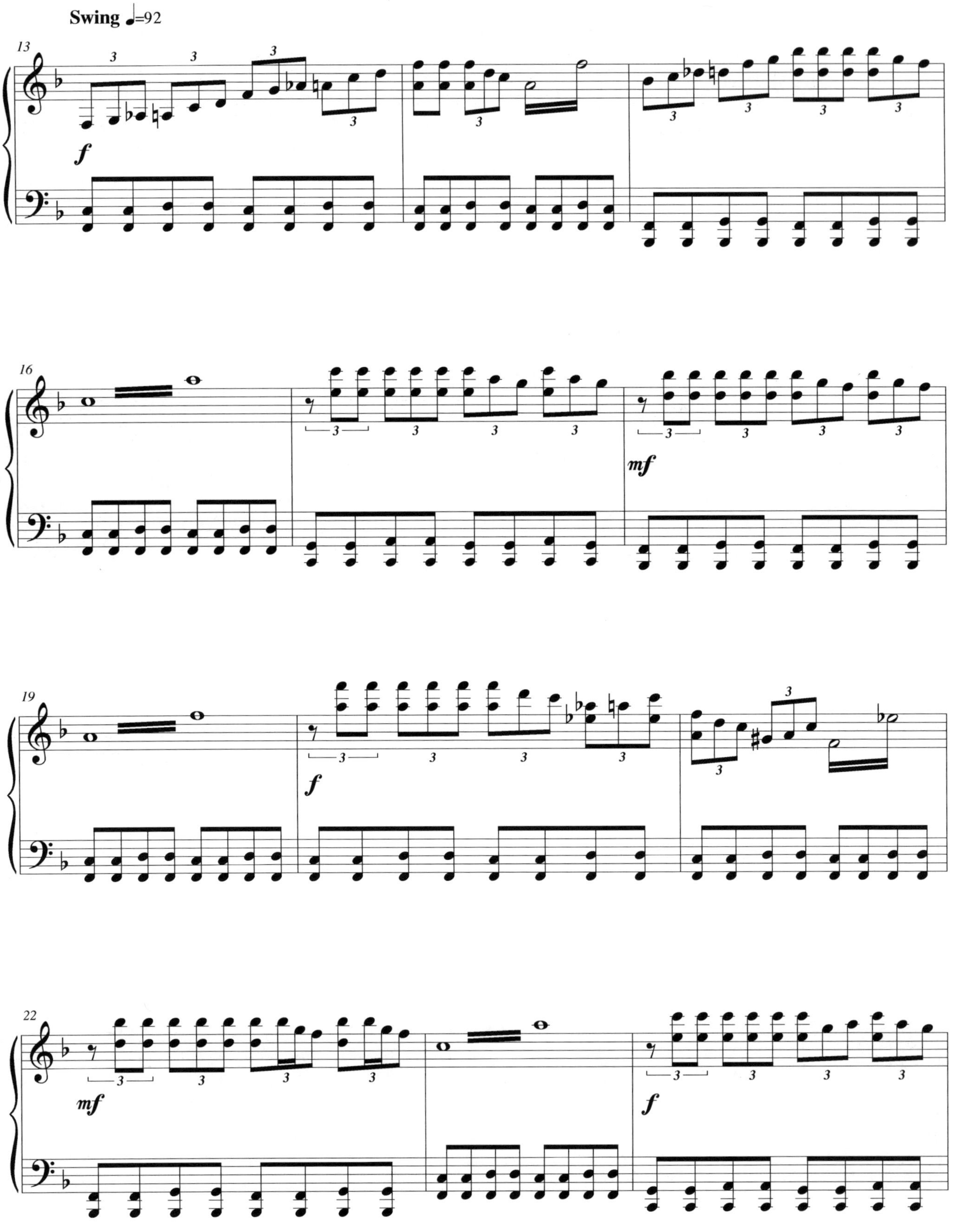
Swing ♩=92

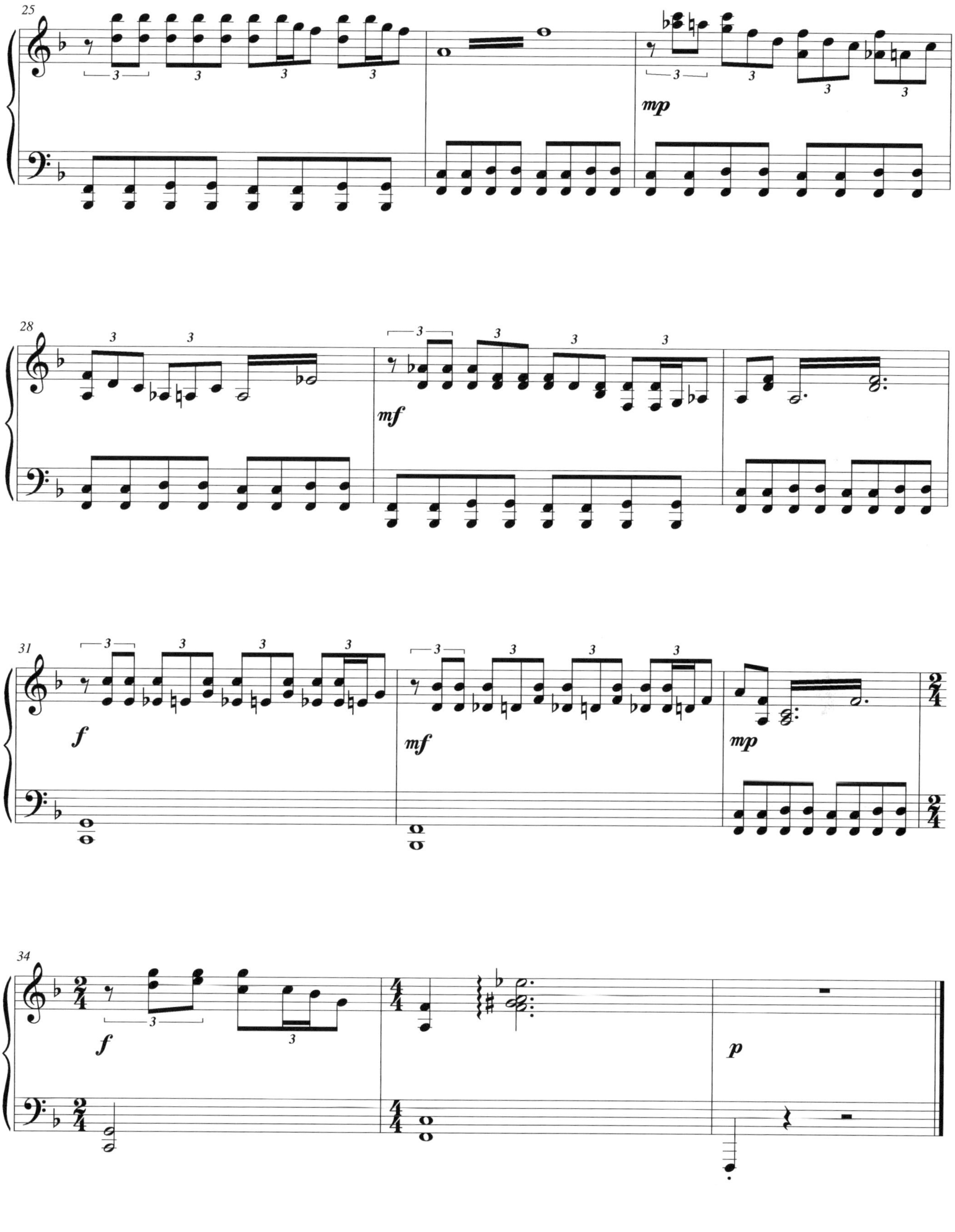
mp
mf
f
mf
mp
f
p

More Reading and Music

If you enjoyed this book, you might enjoy the following books by Kevin G. Pace as well.

Piano Blues: Playing Minor Blues Scales & Songs on the Piano for Moderate Level Pianists:

A book to teach how to play the blues on the piano. The minor blues scales are shown in all 12 keys, each in the following ways: Right hand scale, left hand scale, both hands scale, an easy song in that key, and a more difficult song in that key. Fingerings are shown throughout. Various chords are shown which can be used with the blues scales. This book is intended to teach pianists how to play and improvise using the minor blues scales.

The Comprehensive Book of Modes and Scales: For Piano and Keyboard Players:

Written specifically for classically trained pianists with little knowledge of scales. This book contains over 70 scales and modes including major, minor, jazz modes, pentatonic, bebop, octatonic, exotic, synthetic scales, etc. Each scale is shown with its interesting features, chords that may be used with it, and several ways to think of the scale. Each scale is shown in all 12 keys.

The Comprehensive Book of Chords: For Piano and Keyboard Players:

Written specifically for pianists, but could be used by anyone. This book contains over 100 chords. Each chord is shown with its interesting features, scales that may be used with it, and several ways to think of the chord. Suggestions for voicings of these chords are given. Chords of up to eight tones are presented. Each chord is shown in all 12 keys. Over 130 pages.

Rock 'n Boogie Blues books 1 through 5 (piano solos):

Fun, entertaining, original piano solo music. Written with various boogie basses and blues harmonies. Moderate to advanced in difficulty. Excellent music for piano lessons, recitals, or personal enjoyment.

All books available on Amazon.com or PaceMusicServices.com

Made in the USA
San Bernardino, CA
23 May 2017